INTRODUCTION

When I was about six years old, I bought my first lizard, a green anole. I was proud of my little "chameleon," and I kept it in a converted 5-gallon aquarium. I went out into the backyard and chopped out a little square of sod that I used to cover half of the bottom of the tank. The other half

hope that maybe what I've learned since then will help you to avoid the mistakes I made.

I realize that many of you who will read these words are young people. Maybe you have received an anole as a gift, as so many young animal lovers do, and you don't know any-

Green anoles depend upon you to give them proper care and feeding. Photo by Elaine Radford.

was water. I had a screen top on the tank, but no light.

At first my little lizard was perky. I fed it flies that I caught outdoors, and I chopped up a few earthworms for it. (It didn't eat the earthworms.) I did have to replace the sod in its cage a lot, though—it got kind of brown and soggy after a few days. My parents were not very happy about the little square patches of bare ground that mysteriously began appearing in their neatly manicured lawn.

I handled the anole a lot, and I thought it was getting "tame." Suddenly, one morning it was dead, and I was heartbroken. What had I done wrong?

Just about everything, actually. And that's why I'm writing this book. I didn't have the right information when I obtained my first anole, and my ignorance killed that poor lizard. I

thing about how to keep it. Maybe you are an adult who wants a pet that is a little different. No matter who you are, this book has one main goal—to help you keep your anole alive and healthy. Many anoles are sold every year, and it has to be admitted that a pretty fair percentage of them die. This doesn't have to be, and I hope that this book will help to reverse the trend. Information is the key.

I will try to keep things simple and to the point. An anole can be a fascinating and worthwhile pet that will introduce you to the beauty of all reptiles and amphibians. If you enjoy your anole, I hope that it will lead you to keeping other "herps," as we call all reptiles and amphibians. There are colorful snakes, fantastic frogs, charming turtles, and many more discoveries awaiting you.

Green anoles and their relatives are great fun to keep, and they are a great introduction to the wonders of the world of reptiles. I hope you enjoy them and are successful in keeping and breeding them.

Watch your anoles. Study them. Keep notes on their behavior. Read every book you can lay your hands on. If there's one in your area, join a local herp society. If there isn't one, consider founding one. Encourage the captive breeding and conservation of all reptiles and amphibians. Let your friends and family see how much you enjoy your pets—the curiosity will be contagious. Try to help others understand the vital role that anoles and other reptiles and amphibians play in natural habitats. Herps have gotten a lot of bad press from the ignorant, and myths about them abound. Help others to see the truth.

In short, take your hobby seriously, but do have fun at the same time. In the long run, both you and your pets will be better for the experience.

GLOSSARY

Acclimation—Settling-in period for new herps, preferably in a sterile cage separate from the eventual display cage.

Arboreal—Tree-dwellers, climbers.

Autotomy—Programmed loss of a limb as a defense mechanism, as in a lizard's breakaway tail.

"Head bob"—Territorial display in anoles consisting of rapid upand-down thrusts of the head.

Herpetology—The study of reptiles and amphibians.

"Herp"—Slang collective term for reptiles and amphibians.

Hygrometer—Device for measuring relative humidity.

Iguanid—A member of the lizard family Iguanidae; includes anoles.

"Loading"—Feeding insects a high-nutrition diet just prior to feeding them to herps.

Metronidazole—Wide-spectrum anti-protozoan drug.

Noosing—Collecting method for catching small lizards.

Photoperiod—Length of daylight exposure.

Pineal eye—Light-sensitive organ atop head of anoles; regulates activity and reproduction.

"Pushups"—Territorial display in anoles consisting of up-and-down motion of forebody.

Throat fan—Erectile cartilage from hyoid bone on neck of anoles that displays colorful throat skin; used by male anoles in courtship and territorial display.

UV—Ultraviolet light; energetic shortwave radiation important in vitamin D_3 synthesis.

WHAT IS AN ANOLE?

First things first. Anoles are reptiles, with scaly skin and fully shelled eggs that distinguish them from the amphibians that are one rung lower on the evolutionary ladder. The study of reptiles and amphibians is called *herpetology*.

Reptiles are usually called "cold-blooded," but that's really not fair. They just have a different approach to heating their bodies than "warm-blooded" critters like you and me.

Any food an animal eats produces energy. This energy can be used for lots of things—growth, movement, reproduction, and more. Mammals and birds—warm-blooded animals—use a big portion of their total food energy to keep the body warm. This means they are always raring to go, but the disadvantage is that less energy is left over for other functions. Reptiles warm the body by basking in the sun, and don't "waste" their food energy to do it. When fully warmed by the sun, most reptiles have a body temperature—and activity level—pretty close to that of a mammal. At night, or during cold weather, reptiles don't fight it the way mammals do—they simply go dormant and wait for the sun to return. Because of this frugal use of energy, a reptile needs far less food than a mammal or bird of the same size. So looking down on the "primitive, cold-blooded" reptiles is a disservice. From a certain point of view, they're more efficient than we are.

Anoles are lizards of the family Iguanidae, a huge family that includes the green iguana and over 550 other lizards, almost all of them in the New World. The iguanids, in fact, comprise the vast majority of New World lizards. If you were a taxonomist, a scientist who studies the relationships between animals and names them, you would say the family Iguanidae represents a traditional, or "lumper," point of view.

The opposite of the "lumper" philosophy is the "splitter." In 1989, two herpetologists, Frost and Etheridge, published a scientific paper in which they said that the big family Iguanidae was not really a natural group of closely related lizards, so they proposed splitting it

Anoles are reptiles; they are also lizards. They are cold-blooded and are members of the family Iguanidae. Photo by Michael Gilroy.

Anoles are small iguanid lizards which range from 4 to 20 inches. They are wonderfully adapted to climbing. They can run and climb straight up, straight down and even sideways as this green anole is doing. This ability derives from their specialized toes. Photo by Elaine Radford.

into eight separate families that are more natural groupings. The jury's still out on whether they are correct, but if you accept this "split," it puts the anoles into the family Polychridae.

Anoles are small as iguanid lizards go, ranging from 4 to 20 inches. In most species, half to two-thirds of the total length is the tail. Anoles are mostly arboreal (tree-climbers), and they need that tail for balance.

Anoles have another incredible adaptation for climbing—their toes. An anole can run up a vertical tree trunk, hang upside down on a leaf, or even climb glass—and it's all in the toes. They are flattened and have tiny ridges on the bottoms, and these ridges are marvelous. Most people who watch an anole run across a windowpane assume that the feet have some sort of suction cups. Not true! If you magnify the toe ridges very highly, such as under an electron microscope, you will find that they are covered with tiny hooks. And glass, smooth as it looks, is not smooth at all—under magnification, it has thousands of tiny projections. The hooks on an anole's toe ridges catch on the tiny, unseen projections on glass or any other smooth surface. An anole is like a tiny mountain climber, putting hooks into crevices and hanging on.

Anoles have other fascinating anatomical features. One is the *throat fan*. Attached to the throat is a stiff rib of cartilage that the anole can flare outward. When the cartilage is erect, it stretches the skin of the throat into a flat half-circle. The

Green anoles can change colors quickly, but they are NOT chameleons. Their main color changes are from brown to green and vice versa. It takes about one minute for a brown anole to change to a green anole. Photo by Michael Gilroy.

All anoles have throat fans. The males have larger throat fans than females. The fans are used mainly in territorial disputes. Photo by Michael Gilroy.

throat fan makes the anole's head look much bigger, and it is also brightly colored—usually red or orange. All anole species have throat fans, and they are usually better developed in the males, who use the fan-flaring display to intimidate other males. This way, a strong male claims a territory and the right to mate with local females. All anoles are territorial to some degree.

Another curious anatomical feature of anoles, which they share with many other lizards and snakes, is the

Facing page: Green anoles, *Anolis carolinensis*, get their water by lapping small droplets which form on plants and flowers. Water is a vital necessity for green anoles; they drink about half a teaspoonful per day. Photo by Michael Gilroy.

pineal eye. This is an enlarged scale on the top of the head that actually contains a rudimentary third eye. It does not form an image, but it can sense light and darkness. It is a built-in timer that is intimately tied to the lizards' endocrine glands. In other words, it sets the lizards' biological clocks. When it senses that days are growing shorter, it signals the lizard that it is time to hibernate. When it senses that days are growing longer, added to the stimulus of higher temperatures, it triggers the enlargement of the sex organs and the beginning of breeding activity.

The focus of this book is a very special anole called the green anole. Its scientific name is *Anolis carolinensis.*(In a scientific name, the first

Above: *Anolis garmani*, the Jamaican giant anole, reaches about 11 inches in total length. The females stay a few inches smaller. They are beautiful, majestic animals that move swiftly on almost any surface. **Below:** A newly hatched *A. garmani*. Photos by R. D. Bartlett.

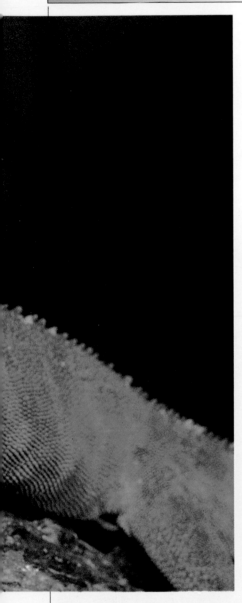

The green anole was once called the "American chameleon" in pet shops. It is NOT a chameleon. Chameleons are very, very weird Old World lizards with opposable toes, prehensile tails, and independently moving eyes. Chameleons are so odd that no one is really sure just what other lizards they're closely related to—but they definitely aren't related to anoles. I'm glad to see that the vast majority of pet shops now call anoles anoles.

Why did they ever call the green anole a "chameleon?" Because chameleons can change color—and so can green anoles. But it's just a coincidence, and while chameleons can change to many colors and patterns (no, they can't do plaid!), green anoles are far more limited—green or brown, and that's pretty much it. The throat and belly are always white. The color changes are not instantaneous, but they are fast. An anole can turn from brown to green, or vice versa, in about a minute.

Even though there are only two colors involved, the color of a green anole can tell you a lot about its mood and condition. You might think a green anole would consciously choose to be brown when it's on a brown background, like the bark of a tree, and green when it's on a green background, say, when sitting on a leaf. Not so! Anoles are brown when they are sleeping or cold, and they turn bright green when they are warmed up and active. There is an exception to the latter rule—an active, warm male anole will turn brown again when he confronts an intruder (i.e., another male anole) in his territory. A sick anole will be brown, but it will be a darker brown than a sleeping/cold anole, and it will not change to green when it warms up.

word is the *genus* and the second is the *species*. A genus may contain many related organisms; a species is unique.) The green anole is a real American, found virtually throughout the southeastern United States—from extreme southeastern Virginia to the Florida Keys, and westward to eastern Texas. (There are populations on a few Caribbean islands and a few Mexican records, but almost all the green anoles in the world are found within U.S. borders.)

As mentioned earlier, green anoles are territorial. Their territorial behavior is fascinating and fun to watch, and so complex that many scientific papers have been written on the subject. We have space to mention only the basics here.

Although female anoles may dominate smaller females, males are far more territorial. Territory size is variable, depending on the terrain and the number of anoles in the area, but based on the anoles I've observed in the wild I would generalize that a male green anole considers about 3-4 feet on any side to be its domain.

When an intruder enters the territory, the resident male moves perpendicular to him and flares his throat fan. In green anoles the throat fan varies from green to red (there are some blue-throats in Florida, and some herpetologists think they should be considered a different species). The redder the fan, the stronger and more dominant the animal. The intruder may return the fan-flaring display. In addition to erecting the throat fan, either or both males may do a "head bob," jerking the head up and down rapidly, or "pushups," in which the whole front of the body is jerked up and down. Usually the interloper will take the hint at this point and back off. If not, the resident male will lunge at him and chase him around until he leaves the area. There is almost never any physical contact—it's mostly ritualized display and bluff. Only occasionally will the combatants get close enough to bite at each other. Rarely, the resident male will lose the

Facing page: Green anoles have very large mouths; they can readily capture and eat living, flying, fast-moving insects. Photo by Michael Gilroy.

Green anoles not only have special toe pads by which they adhere securely even to such surfaces as aluminum and glass, but their toes also grasp as can be seen in this lovely photograph by Michael Gilroy.

battle and be run off by a larger and more dominant intruder, who will then usurp his territory.

Although green anoles climb extremely well, they are not usually seen high up in trees. Rather, they seem to prefer shrubbery, walls, fences, and small trees. They are rarely seen above 15 feet or so, and they are also rarely seen on the ground. They prefer to jump from bush to bush, and they are incredibly acrobatic. Slow-motion photography has shown that they take a big push with the hind legs, arch the spine for additional spring, and launch themselves into the air. While in the air the body is tilted upward about 30°, and the tail is used as a rudder. They can land in almost any position, but most often hit with the front feet first.

Sexing anoles is not difficult. Male green anoles can reach about 9 inches in total length, and the females generally run about two inches shorter. Males also have enlarged

they also get the most girls! Research has shown that females prefer males with bright pink or red throat fans; males with green or white fans are pretty much out of luck if a macho lizard like this lives in the neighborhood. (See the section on breeding for what to do after you've sexed your anoles.)

Green anoles feed on small arthro-

This is a male anole; note the postanal pores. Swellings marking the locations of the hemipenes are visible at the base of the tail below the vent. Photo by Michael Gilroy.

postanal scales (a row of pores on the underside below the vent). Either sex may have a white stripe down the center of the back, but this tends to fade in adult males and is very distinct in juveniles and adult females. We already know that males with the reddest throat fans are most successful in securing territories, but

pods—insects and spiders, mostly. They spend a large percentage of their waking hours hunting—or at least alert to strike at any unwary bug that wanders close.

All in all, the green anole is a marvelously adapted little lizard and, as we shall soon see, makes a fine pet.

COLLECTING ANOLES

Although some readers live within the green anole's natural range and therefore can at least theoretically collect wild stock, in most cases I would not recommend that hobbyists collect their own reptiles. In the case of the green anole I will make an area. For instance, if you live in southern Virginia, at the northernmost limit of the range of the green anole, don't collect them. Populations of any animal at the limit of its geographic range are often small and don't tolerate much disruption (and

Green anoles prefer hiding in shrubs and low trees, awaiting unsuspecting insect food. They are uncommonly found more than 15 feet above the ground. Photo by Michael Gilroy.

exception because they are such common reptiles over most of their range. Still, they will only stay common as long as people care about their welfare in the wild, so collectors do need to follow a few simple rules.

Assuming that anoles live where you live, first make sure that it is legal to collect anoles in your area. The state fish and game department is a good place to start—call or write them and ask whether any permits are necessary to collect anoles for personal use. If there are, get them.

Second, know something about the status of anole populations in your collecting is a disruption, however small). Don't collect if you live, for instance, in an urban area where anoles may be present but hard to find. In short, don't collect anoles unless they are very common. If they're common enough to collect in your area, you shouldn't even have to leave your backyard to find them.

Finally, take only what you can use. If you are keeping anoles for the first time, collect only one or two. Don't give in to the temptation to collect a dozen just because you *can*. They don't do well in captivity if you crowd them.

Alright, enough of the preaching. Where should you look for anoles? Check low, leafy shrubbery and small trees. Anoles often hang out on tree trunks. Even better, though, are brick walls, woodpiles, and wooden fences. When the sun hits these surfaces in the morning you can often find anoles sunning themselves right out in the open, and if they are still a bit cold they can be easily captured by hand.

DON'T GRAB THE TAIL! You'll only get to see a tailless lizard scurry away. Anoles' tails break off very easily as an adaptation for escaping from predators. This is called *autotomy*. The blood vessels at the break seal quickly, and the lizard will be none the worse for its loss, in the long run. The anole will soon grow a new tail, but it will not be as nice as the original. When you're trying to catch an anole by hand, don't try to grab it with your fingers. Instead, try to *gently* slap a cupped hand over the entire lizard. It helps if you place your hand's shadow over the anole while you are still several feet away. If the shadow of your hand crosses the anole when you are closer, the lizard will probably spook.

Another method for catching anoles (and many other lizards) is *noosing*. This is my favorite method; I was usually too slow to catch them by hand. Get a pole about 4 feet long—a stick, fishing rod, or broom handle works nicely—and make a slipknot in the end of a single strand of very thin copper wire (you can get it from an old electrical cord). Some

A closeup of the remarkable toes by which the green anole can move in any direction with speed and assurance. The ridges contain tiny hooklets that catch on minute imperfections that are present even in a smooth surface such as glass. Photo by Michael Gilroy.

people use monofilament fishing line, but I prefer the copper wire because its stiffness will hold it still in light breezes, but it is still flexible enough to make an effective noose. Slide the knot up the wire until you have made a noose just a little wider than an anole's head—about a half-inch-diameter noose should do nicely. The noose should hang about 6 to 8 inches off the tip of the rod. Believe it or not, an anole is usually so preoccupied in watching you that it will not notice as you stretch out your pole and slip the noose over its head. A quick tug closes the noose, and presto! You have captured an anole.

Facing page: If you are going to collect your own anoles, be very careful. DO NOT GRAB THEM BY THE TAIL, or you'll see the anole run away while you have a wriggling piece of tail in your grasp. Use a noose as described in the text. Photo by Michael Gilroy.

Anoles can even cling handily to an unstable surface like this leaf. Photo by Michael Gilroy.

Quick, now, grasp it gently behind the head, loosen the noose, and place the anole in your collecting container. Beware, anoles will bite!

An ideal collecting container is a cloth bag of some sort. (I like to use an old pillowcase.) Basically, you want something that's breatheable and opaque. Don't use glass jars, because they are transparent, and a captured anole may "freak" a bit if it can see out. An old coffee can with a perforated plastic lid will work, but it can get hot on a sunny day (so can the glass jar). Transport your anole home as quickly as possible; the less time you spend out in the field, the less stressed the lizard will get.

CHOOSING AN ANOLE

Most of you will not be collecting your own anoles. So, when you're standing in the pet shop and looking at a cage filled with anoles, how do you choose a healthy one? Selecting a healthy anole is at least half the battle in keeping it successfully.

waking hours. Don't ever buy a mottled, dark brown anole. These poor creatures are really on their way out, and a dead giveaway (no pun intended) is the presence of a black patch behind the eye.

Speaking of the eyes, they are also

The green anole in the center is molting. Molting is a natural phenomenon for anoles, and the lizards will often eat part of the shed skin. Photo by Isabelle Francais.

Be suspicious of anoles kept in crowded cages. The stress of constantly battling for food, water, and territory can take its toll. Be also wary of anoles kept in cages without adequate heat and lighting. Look at the cage substrate—a dirty cage is the number one sign of lackluster care on the part of the keeper.

Look for an anole that is alert. It should look at you as you approach the cage. It may even jump around and attempt to hide from the threat it perceives you as. Anoles have excellent eyesight and are always interested in what is going on around them, even outside the cage, so one that does not acknowledge your presence may be ill.

Look at color. Healthy anoles that are being kept at the right temperature are bright green during their

a very good indication of an anole's overall condition. The eyes should bulge slightly from their sockets. If they are sunken in it means the animal is dehydrated, which usually happens when an anole gets too weak to eat or drink. An anole with sunken eyes is often—literally—just hours away from death.

Anoles that are malnourished begin to show it quickly in the pelvic girdle (hip region) and tail. Well-fed anoles show only the faintest outlines of their bones, but a starving anole will have the lines of the pelvic bones clearly visible beneath the skin. The tail develops a kinked appearance as the muscles atrophy and the skin hugs close to the vertebrae. Even the vertebrae along the top of the back and at the base of the skull may be apparent. The ribs stick out to a grotesque degree. I think you get the idea—a starving anole is really just skin and bones, because all of the fat and most of the muscles have been consumed.

You will want to check for ticks and mites. A tick will appear as a dark, raised, scablike spot. Mites will look like specks of paprika or red dust. Check for these annoying pests at the bases of all the legs, around the neck, and around the eyes and vent. In short, anywhere there is a fold or cavity in the lizard's skin is a good place for ticks and mites to get established.

Check the anole carefully for any sign of injury. A recently broken tail or missing toes (there should be five on each foot) are prime spots for infection. Although anoles can easily survive such injuries, you're better off if you start with a whole anole.

Of course, you, or more likely, a pet shop employee, will have to handle the anole to check for parasites and injuries. The anole will not like this and should open its mouth in readiness to bite. If it does not, be suspicious. An annoyed anole is usually a healthy anole.

If you're lucky enough to see the animal defecate (ooh, some luck…) you may be able to tell a little bit about its digestive health. Stools should be firm, not runny, and there should be no visible roundworms (they are probably still there, but too

When selecting your green anole at your local pet shop, check for obvious sings of injury such as broken tails, missing toes, sores, ticks and mites. Only buy a completely healthy anole. Photo by Michael Gilroy.

Every so often a weird color pattern shows up on a green anole. This freak turned up in Texas and was on display at the Houston Zoo. Photo by Paul Freed.

small to see). Greenish loose stools with a lot of mucus and maybe even some blood mean sure trouble. In general, though, you will probably have to wait until the acclimation period at home to examine stools.

Finally, confirm the sex of the anole, especially if you're buying more than one. Remember, males have large postanal pores (just aft of the vent) that are absent in females. Males are also a bit larger than females and have slightly larger heads in proportion to body size. And although both sexes have throat fans, those of males are distinctly larger and more colorful. You can pull the throat fan out with thumb and forefinger—but gently!

If you follow the guidelines above, you should be able to purchase a healthy anole or anoles easily. Evaluate each animal individually, and don't be rushed. A conscientious pet shop will be just as meticulous as you are, and the staff will be happy to help. If they can't be bothered to take the time to help you, or if they won't let you examine each anole as thoroughly as described here, you might consider taking your business elsewhere; there are, after all, plenty of shops that do care. Keep in mind, though, that many pet shops—as a matter of policy and usually for very good reason based on sad experience—won't let you handle their lizards any more than they'll let you chase and catch your own fish from their tanks.

If through some misfortune you still end up with a sick anole, refer to the "Health" section for tips on dealing with some of the more common ailments.

ACCLIMATION

Once you've finally selected an anole or two, don't just dump them immediately into your display cage. It is often helpful to place them in a small quarantine cage for several days to a week. This lets them settle down after being crowded, poked, and prodded in the pet shop. It gives you a chance to observe them carefully under controlled conditions, and perhaps to notice any possible ailments you missed before. Once you have placed them in their display cage, should they prove to be ill you may need to sterilize the cage—a lot of hassle and expense. By acclimating them in a separate enclosure you can reduce the odds of needing to fiddle with the display cage later on.

The acclimation cage can be a 5- or 10-gallon aquarium, a small wire-mesh cage, or, in a pinch, a gallon jar laid on its side with the lid well perforated. Plastic or silk plants will give the anoles a place to hide and also be easy to clean. Make sure to mist the anoles twice daily, and feed them every day after letting them settle in without disturbance for 24 hours.

If you don't have extra tanks lying around, you can acclimate the anoles in what will become their display cage. After the acclimation period, remove them from the cage and place them in a gallon jar for a couple of hours. If you have assembled all the materials beforehand, you should be able to set up their display cage that quickly.

Photographic backgrounds can add the illusion of depth to a terrarium. Photo courtesy of Creative Surprizes.

Facing page: It is better...much better... to buy an anole which is already acclimated to life in captivity. When you get your first anole place it into your quarantine cage and give it peace and quiet until it becomes accustomed to its new surroundings. Photo by Michael Gilroy.

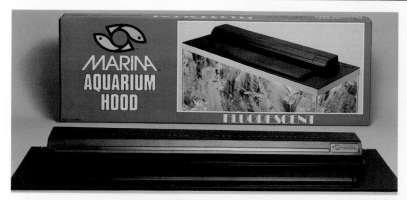

A full hood can be helpful if you want to make an aquarium into an anole terrarium. Photo courtesy of Hagen.

HOUSING

If there's one mistake that most beginning anole-keepers make, it's not giving their pets enough room. Anoles are active and territorial, and they need a lot more space than their small size indicates. One of the most common enclosures adapted as an anole cage is the 10-gallon aquarium, which measures 20 x 10 x 10 inches (length-width-height). Believe it or not, this cage will hold only TWO green anoles, and only if at least one of them is a female. Two males will bully each other mercilessly in this small space until the smaller animal weakens and dies.

Since anoles are so arboreal, even the 10-gallon tank is not ideal (but don't get me wrong—it will work fine for one or two). But if you really want to enjoy viewing your anoles, give them a tank that is not just roomy, but tall. In a tall tank they will do a lot of climbing, and you'll get to see a lot of acrobatic jumping. A 20-gallon "high" tank, which measures 24" x 12" x 16", is terrific, and it's my preferred choice for a pair of anoles. If you'd really like to keep more than a pair, move up to the 55-gallon tank, a real anole condo. Measuring a hefty 48" x 13" x 20", it will comfortably house a male and three or four females. If you're really lucky, it may even be big enough to permit two males to coexist at opposite ends of the tank. No guarantees, though!

Okay, let's assume you're starting small, with a pair of anoles in a 10- or 20-gallon tank, and I'll talk you through the setup.

There are several possible substrates for the floor of the terrarium. The ideal substrate will retain some moisture, as green anoles need about 50-60% relative humidity. Anoles kept in very dry terraria will get dehydrated. Gravel is used by some folks, but I don't like it, because it lets too much moisture and waste creep into hard-to-find spaces where bacteria and fungi can breed like mad. Sand is a little better, but if it is too fine it can irritate the toes of anoles by getting between the ridges. Also, while a little won't hurt, anoles kept over sand may end up accidentally ingesting quite a bit of it. This

Facing page: The anole cage should be provided with living or plastic plants, a piece of clean wood, and lots of space for the anole to move about.

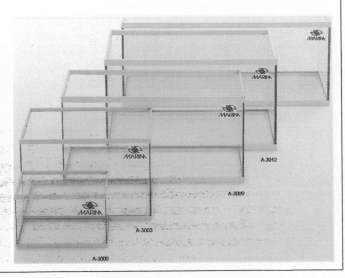

Aquariums come in many sizes. They make the best homes for anoles since they protect the animal from drafts and cats and allow you to view the animal no matter where it is. Photo courtesy of Hagen.

can be dangerous, although I personally feel that sand is a good substrate for many herps. Corncob, commonly used as a reptile bedding, is of questionable value here. It's very unnatural-looking, and while it does absorb a lot of moisture, it also dries quickly, making it hard to maintain a proper humidity level. Some people also claim that if accidentally ingested it swells and causes digestive blockages, but I'll reserve judgment on whether this is true, since I've never used corncob. I just don't like the look of it. Topsoil is a good substrate if the cage is heavily planted. You do have to be careful not to get it too wet, but the plants will help to recycle some anole waste matter.

Perhaps the best anole substrate is bark mulch. Some say that orchid bark is preferable to other types, but I've had good luck keeping a variety of reptiles and amphibians on pine bark mulch. Bark mulch will retain a good deal of humidity, but it is also loose enough that air circulates well through it, keeping stagnant spots to a minimum. A relatively thin layer of topsoil under a generous quantity of bark mulch will give live plants a friendly environment in which to take root.

Make plenty of allowance for the arboreal nature of your anoles. They don't appreciate being earthbound. Lots of wooden limbs and branches should be placed in the terrarium, and they should run at all angles— front to back, top to bottom, side to side. They not only provide needed exercise by letting the anoles run and jump, but they also serve as convenient territorial boundary markers. You'll see how this works as your anoles select a favorite branch or group of branches. And although they don't spend a great deal of time on the ground, you can make the floor of the terrarium interesting by adding rocks and logs.

Plants are a lot of fun. Your anole terrarium can be a miniature garden, and if you have a green thumb there are lots of possibilities open to you. One of the best plants you could pick is a philodendron. They're pretty— one variety even has leaves that are variegated in green and gold—plus they are almost indestructible. Plant a small philodendron in each rear

View your anole as often as possible to ensure it is not stressed by inadequate housing facilities. Remember that anoles like to climb; they are not earthbound animals but are arboreal climbers of trees and bushes. The idea is to make a beautiful terrarium as well as one that satisfies the needs of your anole. Photo by Michael Gilroy.

corner of the terrarium and you will quickly see them fill in the remaining space. Their leaves will also vine around the exposed branches, giving them a more lively appearance. You will soon have to prune back the philodendrons (the cuttings root easily in water and can then be potted to give to friends).

Another good plant is English ivy. The indented leaves are interesting in shape. Ivy grows with amazing speed and also has a creeping habit, winding around bare branches. The leaves are not quite as tough as those of a philodendron, but they are tough enough for small lizards like anoles. This is another plant you will have to prune on a regular schedule.

One more creeping plant that is nice for contrast is wandering Jew, which has attractive green-and-purple leaves. It tends to grow along the ground more than the others and probably won't climb to the same extent.

One plant I particularly like is schefflera. There is a "big-leaf" and a "small-leaf" variety. The big-leaf is a good-sized plant that won't fit into any but the largest terraria, so you should probably go with the small-leaf variety. The five-part compound leaves are bright green. The leaf stalks grow vertically or horizontally, and the plant is not a creeper; rather, it will form a small bush. The leaves of schveffleras are particularly springy—very good for the active anoles.

Bromeliads are very good in the anole terrarium. Many nurseries refer to bromeliads as "air plants." Most do not root in the soil, but attach themselves (non-parasitically) to tree limbs or bark. Small bromeliads can be anchored to wooden branches with rubber bands. In time, they will attach firmly and the rubber bands can be removed.

This is what the inside of a 20-gallon aquarium, suitably equipped for an anole, should look like. Living or plastic plants make the terrarium pleasing to look at as well as comfortable for the anole. Photo by Richard Haas.

Placing your green anole into the terrarium should be accomplished in a gentle manner. DO NOT GRASP THE ANOLE BY THE TAIL. Get a firm grip on its body and slowly release it. Be sure the anole doesn't jump out of the terrarium as you release it. They are difficult to recapture. Photo by Michael Gilroy.

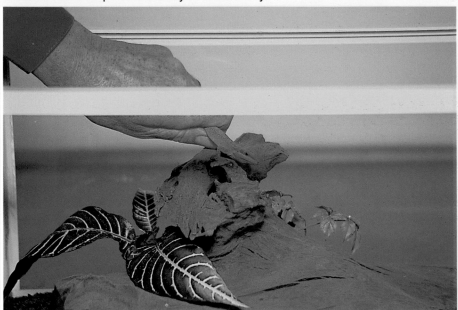

"Air plants" (bromeliads) can be attached to pieces of wood with a rubber band or monofilament nylon fishing line.

This interesting accessory looks like the usual log but it is also heated! Photo courtesy of Tetra/Second Nature.

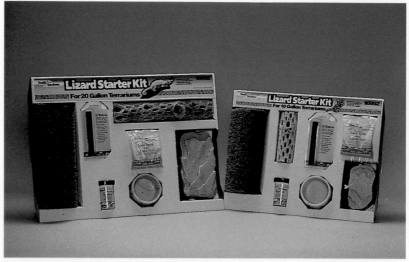

Prepackaged kits are available that include the essentials for starting a lizard terrarium. Photo courtesy of Tetra/Second Nature.

An ideal anole set-up might look something like this. Included are bromeliads and running water.

Small ferns can be used to decorate the floor of the terrarium. They tend to be a little flimsier that the other plants described here, so try to keep them out of what you expect to be "high traffic" areas of the cage.

There are many, many other plant possibilities. For instance, some folks like African violets, and they would add a nice splash of color to an anole terrarium. I couldn't say for sure in this case—I have killed more African violets than I care to admit to. It's just a plant I seem to have a black thumb with! Get a houseplant book and visit a local greenhouse, and you will certainly get some terrific ideas for landscaping your terrarium.

Somewhere in the cage you should have a thermometer and hygrometer (which measures relative humidity). There are electronic models that will give you digital readouts on panels mounted on the front of the terrarium, with their small sensors hidden inconspicuously behind plants or other decor. These models are often expensive, though, and many of you will prefer the less expensive dial-style units. It's up to you, but it is important to be able to monitor both temperature and humidity accurately.

It is necessary to know the temperature INSIDE your terrarium. The digital thermometers made by Hagen attach to the glass and allow you to monitor the temperature.

If you want to go into anoles in a big way you can release some inside a greenhouse. First you start a garden growing, then you add the anole(s). Photo by John Marks.

An artist's rendition of a log which has been decorated with plants to make it more appealing for your green anole.

Left: A terrarium lining can be successfully used for insuring proper cleaning and sanitation in your terrarium. Photo courtesy of Four Paws.

Now that you're done setting up the inside of the cage, get a wire mesh lid. The mesh squares should be ¼ inch. Anything larger may let the anoles escape or, even worse, get stuck halfway. Smaller mesh may also trap them. Aluminum window screening is especially bad. Anoles love to climb on it, but they will sometimes snag a toenail in it to the point that they pull off a toe when struggling to free themselves. The long, slender toes of anoles break off much easier than you'd think!

LIGHT AND HEAT

The cage is now decorated and covered. Now we consider the vital topics of light and heat, which overlap to some degree, as you'll see.

Just above the cage lid, across the entire length of the cage, you should run a full-spectrum fluorescent light. These tubes mimic fairly closely the spectrum of natural sunlight. (Remember, sunlight is not white, but is composed of all the colors of the rainbow—these colors are the *spectrum* of the sunlight.) Most important in the full-spectrum fluorescent tubes is a type of light you can't even see: ultraviolet. UV light is high-energy radiation that helps animals synthesize their own vitamin D_3, which is intimately tied to calcium metabolism and thus promotes healthy bones and teeth, among other things. It should be noted, however, that all fluorescent tubes degrade with time—their spectra will shift, and UV output and overall brightness will decrease. In general, you should replace the tubes about every six months, but refer to the manufacturer's specifications to be absolutely sure.

In addition to the fluorescent light, you must provide an incandescent light as a source of heat. It should shine over only one corner. This lets the anoles regulate their internal temperature by moving away to the cool end of the cage if necessary. Use a spotlight, as a normal round bulb does not concentrate the heat over one area as effectively. A 100-watt

Another concept in terrarium arrangement is a large piece of bark (for the anole's climbing habits) along with suitable plastic plants. Pet shops carry many aquarium plants made of plastic, and these can be adapted for terrarium use. Photo by Susan C. and Hugh Miller.

spotlight should do the trick. Please be sure that the receptacle is rated for such a hot bulb, as many typical household lamps are limited to only 60-75 watts. Aim the spotlight at a large branch, rock, or other spacious bit of decor that can serve as a basking site. You will need a thermometer to measure the air temperature at the basking site. It should be about 90°F. You will probably need to play around with

the normal round variety, to spread out the heat a little more. Keep the cage away from drafty areas, but you can let the temperature drop to as low as 60-65°F by night.

A heating alternative used by some people, but which I personally find just a little too cumbersome, is to run heat tapes under the soil or place a heating pad under the whole terrarium. If you go this way, make sure that the heating device you buy is

Natural-looking devices can be functional in supplying the necessary heat that anoles require for their health and welfare. Photo courtesy of Four Paws.

the spotlight a bit, varying the angle and distance from the basking area, before you get it just right. For this reason, I find that a gooseneck lamp, which can be easily moved up, down, and around, is perfect.

The air temperature over the rest of the terrarium should be about 78-85°F. The warmth radiating from the basking spotlight and the fluorescent lights will probably do this effectively, but if you need to boost the temperature a bit more, you can add a second incandescent light of 60-75 watts—

Facing page: This anole is probably just cold, but this photo shows the black wedge behind the eye that is persistent in sick, weak anoles. If your anole always looks like this, it's in trouble! Photo by Michael Gilroy.

safe for your application. For instance, fires have been caused by herp hobbyists using heat tapes that were originally designed for keeping water pipes from freezing; the tapes overheated. Some years ago I used a garden heat tape in a snake cage, and it melted. In this case there was no fire and no cooked herps or cooked herp hobbyist, but I offer it as an example of what *not* to do! Any inside heater must have a thermostat and must be run under a substrate of even consistency. For instance, if the heat tape runs under topsoil and then through gravel or another medium that has a different consistency, or if part of the tape is accidentally exposed to the air, hot spots can develop where the tape may melt. The same goes for a heater placed outside the cage, for instance, attached to the bottom. Overheating the glass will cause it to crack. Again, a thermostat is a must.

For these reasons, I prefer to use

This anole is probably an old male, judging from the nape crest. Photo by Elaine Radford.

only incandescent lights as my heat sources, and I achieve the desired temperatures by varying their number and their distance from the cage.

The length of the day is one of the factors anoles use to set their "biological clocks." (Remember the pineal eye!) For most of the year you should keep the lights on for fourteen hours a day. Shorter daylengths have their uses, however—see the section on breeding for more details.

Automatic timers, easily found in any hardware store, will make photoperiod regulation a breeze. Trust me, it can really get to be a hassle to remember to turn on the lights at the same time every day. And if you're inconsistent about the length of time the lights are on each day, the anoles can get "confused," for lack of a better term. They may go off their feed, and if the situation continues they may take ill from the stress.

Using a pair of timers, you can even create an artificial morning and evening. Set your full-spectrum fluorescent lamp to turn on an hour before the incandescent spotlight. This simulates, in a crude way, the gradual increase in temperature and brightness as the sun rises higher in the sky. In the evening, have the incandescent spot turn off an hour before the fluorescent light.

That pretty much describes the setup for a very naturalistic cage. If your funds are limited, or if you prefer a simpler cage to make maintenance easier, here are some tips. Set up the cage using only a 1- to 2-inch layer of bark mulch as a substrate, with no underlying topsoil. Plants are still necessary, but they can be in clay pots to make removal easy. I strongly recommend that you do not omit the full-spectrum fluorescent light; however, if you must, then it is absolutely necessary to ensure that your anoles get vitamin D_3 from the supplement powder you use to dust their insects. A vitamin D precursor is transformed to D_3 in the presence of UV light, but in its absence the D_3 must be supplied orally. Extra heat can be supplied by placing an aquarium heater in a gallon jar filled with water, then placing this combo in the terrarium. Be careful not to let the

Facing page: This green anole is in the middle of a color change from green to brown. The change from brown to green or green to brown takes about one minute. Photo by Michael Gilroy.

Your local pet shop will have a wide variety of plastic plants to enable you to artistically set up your anole terrarium. Photo courtesy of Tetra/Second Nature.

water inside the jar get much over 90°F, and make sure to top off the water inside the jar as it evaporates, as an aquarium heater exposed to air overheats and cracks in just minutes.

If you live in an area where summertime temperatures are mild, you might want to build an outdoor enclosure for your anoles. You can construct a simple frame with plywood and then staple ¼-inch mesh hardware cloth to the framework. (Make sure there are no sharp edges, and make sure the door fits securely enough to prevent the anoles from escaping.) There are several advantages here. One is that you can build a large enclosure very cheaply. Another is that you will probably not have to feed your anoles very frequently. A dish of fruit placed in the cage will attract many flies and other insects on which the anoles can feast. You will also not have to worry about

artificial lighting and heat, but do make sure the cage is not out in full sun for the whole day. It is better to place it in light shade, where shafts of sunlight penetrate here and there. Several large potted plants will give the anoles shelter, and they will likely lay their eggs into soil in the pots. (Collect the eggs promptly, though, because the hatchlings will probably be able to slip through the mesh if they hatch inside the cage.) The disadvantage to this setup is that you have little control over your lizards— they are subject to all the possible parasites and harsh environmental conditions encountered by their wild brethren. In general, I recommend that you try an outdoor cage only if you live in an area where green anoles are native, just in case they or their offspring escape in spite of all of your precautions!

Regardless of the type of cage layout you've selected, there will be some maintenance required. Remove fecal matter as soon as you see it. (Even in a naturalistic cage you should be able to find almost all of it). I like to replace small areas of substrate with fresh material on a rotating basis. For instance, one month you might change the substrate in the right one-third of the terrarium, the next month the center one-third, and so on. This way, even if you miss some waste material, and even if the plants do not recycle all of it, you will have reduced the chances of having the cage become unsanitary. Provide drinking water at least twice daily, if not even more continually. Monitor the temperature and humidity every day (it may help if you jot the figures down in a notebook so that you can track them over time to ensure they stay fairly consistent). You may find that condensation builds up on the inside glass; the water may also leave spots on the

Full-spectrum fluorescent lighting helps reptiles such as anoles produce vitamin D_3. Photo courtesy of Zoo Med.

glass. When necessary, you can remove it simply by wiping evenly from top to bottom with a paper towel. (An important note: never use ammonia-based window cleaners, or any other cleaning fluid, in or near your anole cage. The risk of accidentally poisoning your lizards is just too great.) Feed every day in most cases, or at least every other day. Look for anole eggs buried in the soil and remove them to incubators. Spend a few minutes watching the anoles every day to make sure they are active, alert, and acting normally. Don't shirk your responsibilities; just a few minutes of care each day will greatly reduce the chances of problems later on.

When properly cared for, a naturalistic anole cage is a beautiful accent to your home and is even pretty enough to go right into the living room!

You can appreciate the supple toes and fine scales on this green anole. Photo by Michael Gilroy.

HANDLING ANOLES

In a word, don't. Anoles, for all their charms, are not "cuddly" animals, and really don't enjoy being handled. Obviously, there are a few times when you will have to handle your lizard, especially when you're doing some maintenance inside the cage.

If you do have to move your anole, try to grasp it right behind the head, using a thumb and forefinger. Gently! Use only enough pressure to keep the lizard from squirming and twisting its head around to bite. Close the rest of your hand softly around the body.

Wild or captive, anoles can and will bite. While it's certainly not dangerous, a big anole such as a 7- or 8-inch male can give you a surprisingly powerful nip, and the larger teeth at the rear of the jaws can actually draw a little bit of blood. An anole bite can be dangerous to the lizard itself, though. Anole jaws and teeth are easily injured, especially if you try to forcibly remove the lizard from your finger. If you're bitten by an anole, and it doesn't want to let go (this is pretty common) put it back in the cage and let it get a grip on something with its feet. Usually it will then let go right away.

As mentioned previously, anoles lose their tails VERY easily. This is another good reason not to handle your anoles excessively. There's always the chance you will miss and get the anole by the tail. The wound left by the breaking tail, while not serious in most cases, does offer a nice spot for bacterial and fungal infection. And while the tail will grow back, it will be shorter, darker in color, and often a bit kinked, in comparison to the original. "Original equipment" anole tails are nice and straight and are about ⅓ longer than the anole's head-to-vent length.

There is one more reason not to handle your anole frequently, and it's the most important reason of all: handling stresses the lizard. Stress is a very subtle phenomenon that is only just starting to be appreciated as a cause of illness. Stressed animals are nervous, have poor appetites, and often fall prey to disease. So keep in mind: a stress-free anole is a happy anole! Keep handling to a minimum!

Below: A green anole molting. Photo by Burkhard Kahl.

Facing page: The Cuban or knight anole, *Anolis equestris*. This is a large, aggressive species that often bites if carelessly handled. Photo by M. Panzella.

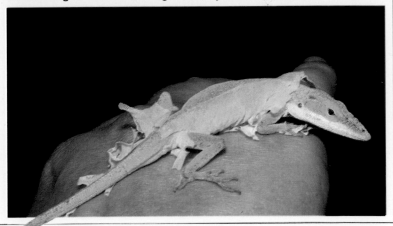

This is *Anolis sagrei*, the brown anole. Note the colorful throat fan. See page 62 for more information.

The bighead anole, *Anolis cybotes,* from Hispaniola. It has also been accidentally introduced into Florida. See page 62 for more information.

FOOD AND WATER

Feeding anoles is not difficult, but there are some tricks to making sure that an anole gets the right kind of food and enough of it.

Green anoles are insect-eating lizards, and rarely consume anything else (more on the exceptions in a minute). Remember the poor anole I killed when I was a kid (back in the Introduction)? Well, anoles don't eat earthworms! And the flies I fed it were only a little bit better. Anoles have a rapid metabolic rate (by day), and my first anole starved to death, unable to sustain itself on the hard-bodied flies and their low nutritive value. You should aim at offering your anole(s) mostly relatively soft-bodied insects, and plenty of them.

Let's go over some of the common insects available for feeding anoles, and look at their pros and cons.

Mealworms (Tenebrio sp.) are the larvae of a small black beetle. They are easily maintained and bred in a medium consisting of grain-based foods: oats, cornflakes. The medium must be kept pretty dry, or fungal infections can kill off the whole mealworm colony. Mealworms are pretty slow-moving, and not all anoles will take them. They also have a lot of chitin (shell, or exoskeleton), and if fed in large quantities can prove hard to digest. Still, some studies of digestive efficiency in lizards indicate that nearly 90% of a mealworm is digested completely, with crickets coming in at about 70%. "Softshells," whitish mealworms that have just molted, are easier to digest and should be fed more frequently than the hard ones. The downside to this idea is that at any given moment, in a colony of several hundred mealworms, you will probably find only several soft ones. Plus, their shells harden and darken to the normal brown color in less than a day. The adult beetles can also be fed to your anoles, but they are very hard-shelled and have a lot less food value than the mealworms they came from.

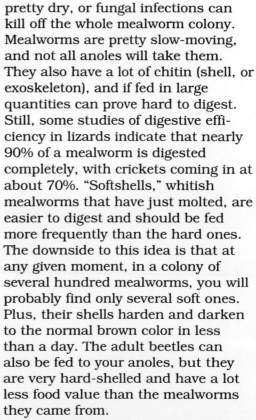

Don't just toss mealworms around the cage and hope your anoles will find them. Most of the mealworms will burrow into the soil and escape. Place a dozen or so in a steep-sided glass dish that is buried flush with the substrate. It will take them a little while to get used to it, but eventually your anoles will learn that this is where the food is, and they'll look for the mealworms in the dish.

Some people claim that if mealworms are not well crushed in a lizard's mouth before swallowing, they can burrow their way out through the stomach wall. Other people claim that this is nonsense. The only reason I mention it here is that I have seen a couple of cases over the years where it looked like that had happened. In other words, a

dead lizard with a hole in its side was found next to a live mealworm. This isn't sure proof, since mealworms will gnaw on dead meat, and there was no sure way to know whether the mealworm ate its way *out* of a live lizard or *into* a dead one. If mealworms do occasionally pull this *Alien* trick on critters that eat them, I certainly don't think it's common, but actually a sort of freak accident. Just be aware of the possibility. And, by the by, I'd like to hear from any readers with stories that more firmly prove or disprove this little bit of herp folklore.

King mealworms (*Zophobas* sp.),

A king mealworm grows to about 2 inches in length and is much heavier than the normal mealworms.

at about 2 inches in length, are about twice as long, and several times as heavy, as a normal mealworm. I would recommend always feeding these as softshells. Otherwise, their care is about the same as for the smaller mealworms, except that they will not pupate unless isolated. If you take several and place them individually into small containers, such as old plastic butter tubs, they will develop into adult beetles that can be used to

Facing page: Green anole making a meal of a cricket.

start a new colony. The same comments apply with regard to their advantages and disadvantages as anole food.

Cockroaches are pretty disgusting, if you ask me. Still, small roaches such as the German cockroach (*Blatella germanica*) are fast-moving, and anoles really seem to enjoy chasing them down. They are very easy to raise and eat just about anything, but have some serious disadvantages. Because they're so quick, they have a tendency to escape, and they are very serious house pests that are nearly impossible to eradicate completely. Also, if you obtain your "feeder roaches" by catching them around the house, there's no telling where they've been. They are definitely disease carriers, and they have often been into some insecticide as well. Some people swear by them as herp food, and you can make up your own mind, but on the whole you might want to skip them.

Waxworms are the larvae of a small moth, and inhabit abandoned beehives. They can be raised on a mixture of beeswax, honey, and oats.

The English field cricket, *Gryllus,* makes excellent anole food. Similar crickets are found all over the world and can also be used. Photo by Michael Gilroy.

Like mealworms, waxworms are slow-moving, but they are much softer-bodied. Feed them to your lizards in a dish. The adult moths are a special treat and will give your anoles a good workout as they chase them around the cage.

Crickets are the Cadillac of live foods. In spite of the debate over whether crickets or mealworms are digested more "efficiently" by lizards, it does seem that fewer cases of digestive upsets (blockages, etc.) result from an exclusive diet of crickets as opposed to one of mealworms. In hardiness, ease of handling, and overall nutritive value, I prefer to use crickets. I fully realize that some may disagree on this point.

Another plus to crickets is that they are fast-moving (but not so fast as to be uncatchable, like roaches). Active insects are really attractive to anoles, and the psychological benefit of the chase should not be overlooked. It really does invigorate anoles to run around after their prey,

DON'T BUG ME! These crickets seem to be having fun on the back of an anole. This is dangerous sport. Photo by Michael Gilroy.

and the activity reduces stress. The bottom line is that exercise is as good for your anoles as it is for you and me. Crickets are available from your pet shop in a wide variety of sizes, from "pinheads" on up to adults about an inch long. An appropriately sized cricket should be about half the length of your anole's head, although your lizards will try to cram down larger ones (don't let them).

Crickets have a couple of major advantages over other foods. They are relatively soft-bodied as insects go, and they have nice fat abdomens that can carry a lot of nutrition.

But just because a cricket *can* carry a lot of nutrition doesn't mean that it does—at first. A cricket, or any other food insect, is only as nutritious as its gut contents. If there's any recent single advance in herp-keeping that I would rate over all others, it's a new emphasis on the importance of "loading" feeder in-

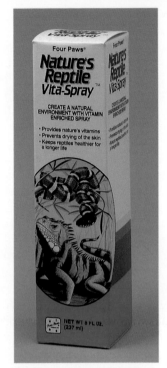

Regular use of vitamin supplements is highly recommended for anoles. Photo courtesy of Four Paws.

I TOLD YOU NOT TO BUG ME!

sects. When I was a kid, you went down to the pet shop, bought your crickets or mealworms, fed them to your herp, and that was that. It led to a lot of malnourished animals. Today, we realize that the most important thing is not so much what you feed the lizard, but what you feed to the food the lizard eats.

Take crickets. To make them a better lizard food, we want to boost their protein, vitamin C, and calcium content (along with smaller amounts of many other vitamins and minerals). There are several possible sources of protein, and some keepers suggest the use of finely crushed rodent food. Another source, and my personal favorite, is tropical fish flake food. Many of these are about 50% crude protein, and the crickets really go for it with gusto. The dry food will get them pretty thirsty, so give them a wedge of fresh orange (adds vitamin C and calcium). They will also eat grated carrot (adds vitamin A and calcium). Lots of other vegetable

matter will be eaten by the crickets, so be imaginative. Here are just a few ideas: potatoes, zucchini, summer squash, apples, peaches, and berries of all kinds. A food I like to feed as an occasional treat is a very small amount of peanut butter. The crickets enjoy it, and I believe the additional fat and protein to be beneficial to lizards, especially young ones still in a rapid growth phase, or that are emaciated.

Keep your crickets in a glass gallon jar, a small aquarium (dry, of course), or one of those "small animal" cages that the pet shops sell (the kind with the slotted plastic tops). Good ventilation is important. High humidity kills crickets in droves. "Load" the crickets for at least 24 hours before you offer them to your anoles. Keeping the food in small, shallow dishes in the cricket cage will make cleaning much easier.

There is one final step before you feed the crickets to your anoles. I call it the "shake-and-bake" step (even though there's no baking involved!).

Crickets love oranges. A thinly sliced orange sprayed with food supplement enhances the food value of the crickets which will soon be fed to the anoles. Photo by William B. Allen.

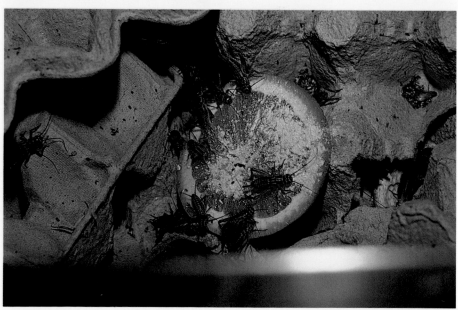

The lubber grasshopper, in various sizes, makes excellent anole food. Grasshoppers are easier to catch than to raise, so try your local pet shop or fishing bait store for local supplies. Usually pet shops can order grasshoppers for you if they don't normally carry them. Photo by Michael Gilroy.

Take four or five crickets and place them in a small plastic bag. Place about a teaspoon of powdered reptile vitamin/mineral supplement into the bag (your pet shop can offer you several good brands, but make sure they are formulated specifically for reptiles and amphibians). Now, gently shake the crickets around in the bag until they are well coated with the vitamin powder. Now they are finally ready to feed to your anoles! You can pinch off the jumping legs (to keep them from hopping out) and place the crickets in a dish as you did with the mealworms, but I prefer to let them run around (exercise for the anoles!).

As long as you put them in only several at a time, your anoles should eat them all.

Your mealworms and king mealworms can be "loaded" in pretty much the same fashion as the crickets, but remove a dozen or so and load them outside the main colony, to avoid introducing too much moisture.

I realize that all this must seem like a lot of trouble to go through to prepare your lizards' food, but it really is not a big deal once you get used to it. Plus, it is an absolute necessity for keeping your herps healthy, so it is well worth the effort. Just do it!

Just a few more notes on food. First, wild foods. You can easily collect in the field a number of small arthropods that anoles will accept. Chief among these are flies, spiders, harvestmen ("daddy longlegs"), and small grasshoppers. While these foods are accepted by anoles—in the of the best is something called "meadow plankton." Take a fine-meshed insect net (check a local pet or hobby shop or order through a biological supply catalog) and sweep it back and forth through tall grass. You'll catch aphids, leafhoppers, small spiders, gnats, and a whole

By checking the base of the tail you can ascertain whether the anole has had enough food. This specimen has a fat buildup at the base of its tail indicating it has been well fed. Photo by Michael Gilroy.

case of the spiders and harvestmen, eagerly so—I would generally avoid them for two reasons: one, they may carry parasites or diseases transmittable to your anoles, and two, they may carry parasite residues and other toxins. In the long run, it's easier and safer to rely on the crickets and mealworms you can buy in your local pet shop or raise yourself.

If you eventually breed your anoles (and I do hope you'll try), you will need some very tiny foods for the hatchlings. And here I'm going to reverse myself on what I just said about wild-caught foods, because one bunch of other tiny goodies that are perfect for baby anoles. There is still the parasite/pesticide threat, but better to take a small risk than not have enough to feed your lizards. An alternative is to raise wingless fruitflies. Fruitfly larvae will eat almost any sort of sweet, overripe fruit, but it is much less messy to order both the flies and a culture medium from a biological supply house (pet shops don't often carry them, but it wouldn't hurt to check).

And although green anoles really like their bugs, they will occasionally consume some vegetable matter, particularly sweet fruity stuff. A fruit puree makes a good treat. Take a soft fruit such as a plum, peach, or nectarine, and add some vitamin powder and a bit of honey. Puree it well in a blender (add some water if the mixture is too thick). When you're done, the mix should be about the consistency of a thick milkshake. When the "fruit shake" is placed in a shallow dish (a laboratory petri dish is perfect), anoles will often lap at it. Use it sparingly, and don't let it sit more than a day—it goes bad pretty fast.

Our last food-related points are important ones: how much do you feed your anole, and how often? It's difficult to give you absolute answers to these questions, but in general, an adult anole will consume four or five medium-sized crickets, or their equivalents (mealworms, etc.), every day. One way to know whether you're overfeeding your anole is if it eats well for several days but then suddenly stops eating. If this happens, let the lizard go hungry for a day and

A green anole searching for insects among dead leaves. It has been successful, as you can see here. Photo by E. Radford.

Anoles can be gluttons. They eat four or five crickets (or equivalent foods like mealworms or grasshoppers) every day! They are CONSTANTLY on the lookout for food. Photo by Michael Gilroy.

then feed a little less in the future (one or two fewer insects per feeding). You will find that if you can feed at the same time every day and at roughly the same spot in the cage (easy if you use a dish), your anoles will anticipate feeding time and stand ready at the "dinner table."

Only slightly less important than food is water. Anoles drink a lot of it. The problem is, they won't drink it from a bowl. Just as they like active food, they seem to enjoy "chasing" their water as well!

An anole will probably drink, on average, about a half teaspoon of water per day. There are several ways to supply this water. Placing an aquarium airstone (connected to a small air pump) into a water bowl will splash small droplets on the nearby glass sides of the cage and on plant leaves. Shiny droplets that catch the light are what anoles will lick at. The down side to this method is that it can be tough to get the splash rate just right; you don't want to soak the whole area around the bowl.

Probably the most common method of supplying water is to mist the tank once or twice daily. Using a clean spray bottle—never one that has ever contained chemicals—lightly wet plant leaves and the glass sides of the terrarium. Getting the anoles themselves wet doesn't hurt either (don't overdo it!). The down side is the same as before—don't soak the terrarium. A wet terrarium is a breeding place for bacterial and fungal diseases. When you mist the cage, it should look like a light dew, not like a rainshower.

If you're really inventive, you might want to build a stream or waterfall. This can look really nice in a large terrarium, but it's beyond our scope here to discuss the mechanical specifics of such a system, which would involve a small circulating pump to move the water. (Just one possible hint: I've seen aquarium powerheads adapted for the purpose.) If you can work it out, though, a constantly moving stream will eliminate any need for you to worry about whether your anoles are getting enough water!

Anoles need water every day. They lap it, as droplets, from plants, thus their terrarium should be misted daily. They will not drink from a water bowl. Photo by Michael Gilroy.

BREEDING

Once you have gotten pretty good at keeping anoles, you may be curious about how to breed them.

In the wild, anoles go into a period of dormancy in autumn. In the northern part of their range they enter true hibernation, but in most areas it tends to be a state of *brumation*. This means the anoles will still come out on warm days, but will spend days to several weeks at a stretch in dormancy. For anoles to breed successfully in captivity, a brumation period is essential.

About October, reduce feedings, and after a couple of weeks, stop feedings altogether. Concurrently, start gradually reducing the photoperiod and temperature. Basically, you're trying to convince the anoles' biological clocks that winter has arrived. After several weeks you want the cage "day" to be only eight hours long, and the temperature only 65-70°F during the "day" and 50-60° at night. You will probably not see much of the anoles—don't disturb them. You can try to offer food if they come out, but don't get upset if they don't eat. If you fed them well beforehand, they should have sufficient fat reserves to weather the winter. After

Anoles during copulation. The male firmly grasps the female, as shown, and swings his body under hers to approximate their genital organs. Photo by R. Allan Winstel.

Copulation between green anoles can take place on the ground or high in trees or bushes. Photo by Michael Gilroy.

four to six weeks of this treatment you can begin to reverse the process—again, do it gradually, over several weeks.

Soon you will be back to the normal 12- to 14-hour "day" and the temperatures in the 80s, and you can get the anoles back on their regular feeding schedule. You should soon notice courtship behavior in your lizards. A male will approach a female with throat fan erect and the head bobbing. The female will probably attempt to run away, but the male will follow her, attempting to stay in a parallel position. If he can catch her (and the ability to catch her in fact signals that the female is receptive), he will bite at the nape of her neck and hold on. At this point both lizards will stop, and the male will wrap his body tightly around his mate's. Most importantly, he will get his tail and vent region wrapped under hers, and soon will insert one of his hemipenes (lizards and snakes have the penis divided into two lobes) into the oviduct for sperm transfer. Mating will last about five minutes. Mating may be repeated numerous times in the days to follow, but fertilization can occur after only one mating.

Females can store sperm and lay fertile eggs for the entire breeding season, which may last 4-5 months. In the wild it's roughly May to September, but by altering temperature and photoperiod you can breed anoles almost anytime you wish.

After mating it is very important to make sure the gravid female anole gets enough calcium, which will be used to secrete strong eggshells. About two weeks after mating, the female should be noticeably heavier and a little bit sluggish. She will look for a moist, warm spot in the substrate and will dig a small hole with her head. In the hole she will lay one egg (rarely, two) about the size of a thumbnail. She will then push the egg into the hole with her snout and cover it up with soil. You have to be very observant or you may miss the event. Look carefully for the female's sudden slimness, then search the substrate for signs of digging. Two weeks later, the sequence will repeat. The female will probably lay approximately ten eggs in the course of one breeding season.

If the terrarium is humid enough the eggs can be left in the terrarium, and it is unlikely that the adults will bother them. Well-fed adults are also unlikely to cannibalize the hatchlings.

Still and all, for the sake of control it is better to remove the eggs to an incubator. A plastic shoebox filled with barely damp vermiculite or sterile sand is ideal. Bury the eggs halfway in the incubator substrate. It is important to position the eggs as they were found. Unlike bird eggs, reptile eggs do not like to be rotated, and inverting the egg may damage or kill the embryo. It is also important for the incubator box to stay at an even temperature—in the case of green anoles, 85°F. Low light levels are best for developing eggs, and a warm closet will often suffice as the place to put the incubator box. Check the eggs once or twice a week to make sure none have gone bad. If you are in doubt, an anole's egg can be "candled" just like a chicken egg: hold it near a light bulb and you should be able to see the developing embryo.

At 82°F, the eggs will hatch in 40 days, give or take several. The hatchlings will be about 2 to 2.5 inches long (1.25 inches head-to-vent length). They will mature at 4-5 inches total length, and they can reach this size in only several months—but they must be hibernated before they will breed. In the wild, green anoles breed at an age of about one year. It is recommended that you not try to push them into breeding early. Precocious breeders often "burn out" at an abnormally early age, and green anoles should be able to breed for several years (probably even longer in the case of males, as sperm production takes far less metabolic energy than egg formation).

Hatchlings must be fed copious quantities of tiny foods—wingless

their insects with vitamin supplements, and it is also recommended to feed the hatchlings fruit puree to which the vitamin/mineral supplement has been added. The babies can even be fed straight honey. As with the adults, make sure the babies are kept under full-spectrum lighting.

When the young males begin to display, it is time to begin dividing up the young anoles, as bitter fighting will soon ensue. You can release the babies if you caught the parents locally, or you can trade them with your friends or the members of a local herp society. Your pet shop may also be interested in your homegrown anoles.

Admittedly, you'll never get rich breeding anoles, but it is still a rewarding endeavor, and I believe that

Green anole females usually lay only one egg at a time. They are the size of your thumbnail. These eggs of a Caribbean *Anolis* were laid in a termite nest. Photo by Dr. Guido Dingerkus.

fruitflies, "meadow plankton," and pinhead-sized crickets. They must also have a great deal of calcium to support normal bone development considering their rapid growth rate. They will require 2-3 times as much calcium as a full-grown adult. Dust

breeding should be the ultimate goal of any animal keeper, no matter how inexpensive or common the creature. Seeing to it that they pass on their genes is, in my opinion, a way of thanking our pets for the pleasure they have given us.

HEALTH

If you have followed my advice in the other chapters, it should be unnecessary to refer to this chapter at all. It's also beyond our scope here to cover every ailment that could affect your anole, but here are some of the most common. We'll deal with the parasites first.

Ticks and mites are less of a problem with anoles than they are with many other reptiles, probably because anoles' tiny scales don't give them much room to attach. (If you really want to see ticks and mites, check out any wild-caught swift, *Sceloporus* spp.) However, considering that most anoles are wild-caught and some are kept under crowded conditions before sale—both of these conditions make the parasites easy to transmit—it's worth being on the lookout for them. Ticks are round-bodied and eight-legged, and they have tiny heads that burrow deeply into the skin of the host. Mites are pretty much the same except that they are much smaller, like dust motes or grains of sand. Check the "armpits" and bases of the hind legs, the neck, and around the eyes and vent—these are all favorite attachment sites. A small magnifier would be helpful.

The traditional means of dealing with mites on reptiles was to place them in a well ventilated sterile cage along with a 1-inch square of "No-Pest-Strip." This worked like a charm, killing all the external parasites in only a few days. It's a shame I can't recommend this method anymore, as the particular pesticide used has

These tapeworms were found inside a *Chamaeleo*. The same sorts of worms can be found in anoles. Photo by Paul Freed.

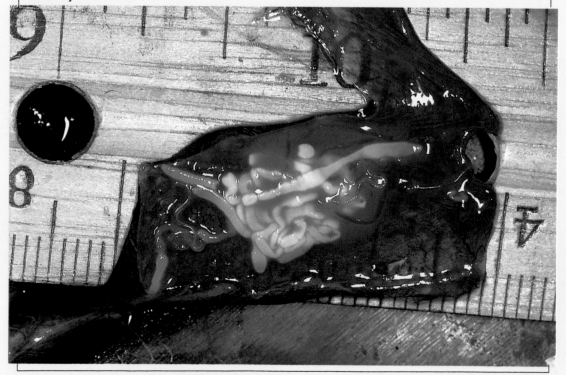

You will need a small microscope or hand lens to see parasites on your anole. If you see one that looks like this, get some permectrin immediately...and use it. Photo by Dr. Frederic Frye.

been banned. There are still pest strips being sold out there, but it seems that they all come from old supplies that have been in storage for a long time, and seem to have lost their effectiveness. Add to that the fact that the chemical involved is pretty toxic to *you*. After all, why do you think they banned it? Don't buy pest strips even if you see them for sale.

Today, the treatment of choice for ticks and mites is called permectrin. It's a synthetic pyrethrin. (Pyrethrin is a plant-derived pesticide that breaks down rapidly and is thus favored by "green"-minded gardeners.) When properly used it is safe and remarkably effective. To obtain it you may need to consult a verterinarian, though it might also be available at a nursery. Don't apply it in the concentrated form in which it is originally supplied. Mix it with distilled water at a ratio of 1:99. That is, one part of permectrin to 99 parts of water. Measure accurately! Fill a small atomizer-type spray bottle with the solution and use it to cover your anoles completely—get it into all those "nooks and crannies" on your lizards. Don't be afraid to get them really wet, but blot off any dripping water when you're done so that the lizards are just damp. Place the lizards back into the sterile cage for a day or two and be sure to keep them warm so they dry completely. Don't let them get chilled while wet.

Worms, usually roundworms, are almost always present in the digestive tracts of wild-caught anoles. Normally they are almost innocuous and not ulturists who use it on anoles just add a small amount to a fruit puree and use it to treat a whole batch of lizards. Piperazine will clear almost all the lizards of worms, but it will also kill a few of the weaker ones. If you are keeping just one or two anoles it will probably not be worth your while to worm them. The good news is that if you followed the directions for choosing a healthy

The snout of one of these green anoles is normal. The other has the beginning of what could develop into mouth rot. Read the text to cure this bacterial infection, which usually results from a wound or injury. Photo by Michael Gilroy.

worth worrying about, but in a stressed anole they can multiply to dangerous levels. Intestinal worms are often the reason why some anoles eat and eat and eat and still lose weight. A drug called piperazine is the most effective means for worming small lizards, but getting the dose just right is difficult. Most herpetoc- anole, it probably does not have enough worms to worry about.

Protozoans are also found inhabiting anole digestive tracts, and they can be eliminated with the drug metronidazole, sold under the trade name of Flagyl. Again, be aware that the treatment is sometimes harsher than the parasites and that weak animals may not be able to take it.

Mouth rot is not often seen in anoles, but it will sometimes occur in an individual that has sustained an injury to the tip of the snout. Mouth rot is characterized by redness and inflammation of the gumline, followed by the presence of a disgusting, foul-smelling cheesy matter that forms as bacteria become entrenched. Treatment involves *gently* debriding the area with a cotton swab soaked in hydrogen peroxide, and then dabbing the area with an antiseptic/antibacterial cream, such as Betadine (an iodine cream), Neosporin, or Polysporin.

Injuries such as amputated toes or broken tails can also be treated by swabbing the area with a disinfectant and applying one of the ointments mentioned above. Remove the lizard to a sterile cage for a few days until the injury scabs over. In its display cage, it may get dirt into the wound and run the risk of infection.

Gastric disturbances are tough to diagnose. There are lots of reasons why an anole may not be eating or may pass loose stools or undigested food. Stress, that common but mysterious bugaboo, is often the cause. Crowded anoles, for instance, are often intimidated by each other and do not eat or digest well. Anoles that are kept at too low a temperature may develop gastroenteritis, which is caused by food literally rotting in the gut because the lizard's body temperature is too low for proper digestion. Too much of one sort of food, such as mealworms, may induce intestinal blockage. Vitamin and mineral deficiencies often manifest themselves first in loss of appetite. In short, when confronted by an anole with obvious gastric problems, you need to evaluate two things: environment and diet. Are the lizards kept in a spacious, warm, clean cage, and do they have a balanced and varied diet? If you can answer yes to both questions, then the advice of a veterinarian or experienced herpetoculturist is needed to isolate other possibilities.

A word about vets. You'll notice that I have mentioned them several times in this book. They are a valuable source of advice, treatments, and medications. It can be tough, though, to find one who is experienced with herps. A call to the nearest zoo may help. If the zoo doesn't know of a local herp vet, ask them if there is a local or regional herpetology society. These clubs are more common than you might imagine, and their members can often steer you to a good vet.

You might be saying to yourself, "I'm not paying a vet to treat an animal that cost me only a few dollars." It's true that consulting a vet will likely cost you at least several times the purchase price of your lizard. But you should ask yourself whether the animal's life is worth more than the retail price. While I know that it's just plain impractical to spend really substantial amounts on anole vet bills, I do believe that there is some level of care worth paying a little extra for—and only you can decide where the cutoff point is for you. I just want you to think about it—just because an anole is inexpensive, that shouldn't make it disposable!

However, the best medicine is prevention. Select a healthy anole at the outset, feed it right and keep it in a proper cage, and you will rarely—probably never—have to worry about treating a sick one.

OTHER ANOLES

Although our discussion up to this point has covered only the green anole, I realize that you can reach a point at which you may wish to give other anoles a try.

While the green anole is the only anole native to the U.S., six other species have become accidentally established, particularly in southern Florida, and occasionally appear in the pet trade. Beyond the one native and the six immigrants to the United States, some 250 species are found from Mexico, throughout the Caribbean, and into the northern half of South America. Most of them are rarely seen in the hobby. In fact, virtually every anole I've seen offered for sale via the usual retail channels has been one of the "big seven," so we'll go through each of them briefly.

Cuban anole, *Anolis equestris.* This is just one heck of an impressive creature. It also goes by the alternative—and appropriate—common name of knight anole. A big male can reach 20 inches! A big chunk of that length is the massive head. Cuban anoles are bright green, with a yellow stripe beneath the eye and another over the shoulder. The scales are large in comparison to those of other anoles (but then, the whole lizard is!) These lizards can bite fiercely and painfully, so handle with care. However, I think they're well worth the effort. They are well established in Miami, Florida, and they distinguish themselves from other anoles by more arboreal habits. You might have thought a green anole was a climber, even though they generally don't get that high into trees—but Cuban anoles sometimes reach the treetops!

Don't keep this lizard in anything smaller than a 55-gallon tank. They are VERY aggressive with each other, so except for breeding attempts it is best to keep only one per cage. (If you have a male, it's worth holding up a mirror to him to get him to flare his tremendous throat fan at his "rival." It's quite a sight!) They do get along pretty well with other big lizards of similar environmental needs, though. Many people house them with green iguanas, for instance.

A hatchling Cuban anole, *Anolis equestris.* Photo by R. D. Bartlett.

By the way, *don't* keep them with your green anoles. The giant has no respect for family and will happily make a meal out of its little cousins.

Like all other anoles, Cubans are active and have a high metabolism, and they are often seen in pet shops in a pretty emaciated state. It takes a lot of food to keep this species in top form. Start off with crickets—lots of them (well gut-loaded and dusted with vitamin powder, of course.) Full-grown grasshoppers are a good food also (adult lubber grasshoppers, see photo on page 47, of the southern U.S. are especially good because of their large size). To really put bulk on a Cuban anole, though, you should feed them occasional small mice. "Fuzzies" or "hoppers," baby mice that are just starting to get some fur, are the right size. Newborn mice ("pinkies") are too small, and an adult mouse just a bit too big (and potentially dangerous to the anole if it decides to fight back). Moisten the hindquarters of a mouse and dip it in vitamin powder just prior to feeding. Curiously, Cuban anoles are also known to consume large chunks of fruit. They will sometimes eat fruit cocktail from a bowl, and some specimens are inordinately fond of grapes.

If you have the room and can keep it well fed, a Cuban anole is definitely a striking and rewarding subject for the hobbyist.

Jamaican giant anole, *Anolis garmani*. This is a very pretty lizard. It is one of the giant anoles, even though it doesn't get anywhere near as big as *A. equestris*, and it is also centered in the Miami area. Males can reach 11 inches, with the females a couple of inches smaller. A male is bright green over the whole body; there are sometimes faint bands on the flanks. There is a distinct crest of sawtooth like scales running from the top of the neck onto the tail. The throat fan is bright yellow and may be orange in the center. Females are also green, but normally lack bands and instead have a row of dots running down the back. This is also a very arboreal species. Care is generally the same as for the Cuban anole, except that Jamaican giants are less likely to take vegetable matter (though it does happen).

A pair of *Anolis garmani*, the Jamaican giant anole. Photo by R. D. Bartlett.

Brown anole, *Anolis sagrei*. This lizard has been so widely introduced that it is hard to know what its original range was. It is now found in most of Florida and the extreme southern tip of Texas. These animals probably invaded the U.S. as stowaways on freight vessels from the Caribbean. In fact, these hardy lizards travel so well that a friend of mine caught one in a parking lot in Trenton, New Jersey! How it got there is anyone's guess. Males can reach almost 9 inches, though about two-thirds of that is tail. Females, on average, are about half the size of males. Brown anoles are brown (surprise!); males may have a few whitish flank bands and females often have a diamond pattern on the back. Both sexes have a white stripe on the throat, formed by the edge of the throat fan, which may be brown, them in the same way as green anoles, and if you have a spacious cage you can even keep them with green anoles. Brown anoles spend most of their time on the ground, though. They can climb, but they don't like to, preferring to dash under logs or bark when threatened. They can be kept a little drier than green anoles.

Bighead anole, *Anolis cybotes*. (Illustrated on page 40.) Males reach about 8 inches, females only about 5. Even though this is not a big anole, males have a surprisingly regal appearance. There is a dorsal crest, but much more impressive is the nuchal (neck) crest, which gives the head an impression of greater size and inspired the common name. Males may have green patches near the forelegs, but overall are some shade of brown. The throat fan is

The brown anole, *Anolis sagrei*. Photo by R. T. Zappalorti.

yellow, or even red.

Brown anoles are excellent terrarium pets. To tell the truth, they even exceed green anoles in adaptability. (In fact, they seem to be crowding out green anoles in some parts of Florida.) You can care for yellow. Originally native to Hispaniola (the island that contains Haiti and the Dominican Republic), *A. cybotes* is now common in southern Florida. Habits and care are roughly similar to those of the brown anole.

The bark anole, *Anolis distichus*. Photo by R. D. Bartlett.

Bark anole, *Anolis distichus*. This is a teensy anole, but kind of cute. It reaches 5 inches, but with over half that being tail, we're talking *little* here. It is mottled gray with thin, rearward-pointing black chevrons on the body and dark bands on the legs and tail. The throat fan is yellow. It is very fast and very arboreal, and is rarely kept by hobbyists although it should do well if supplied with mealworms and small "pinhead" crickets. It will mix well with small green anoles and bark anoles. Cage conditions are as for green anoles. It is originally from the Bahamas and Hispaniola, and is now established in—surprise!—Miami.

Puerto Rican crested anole, *Anolis cristatellus*. Males reach 7 inches (4 inches of that is tail), and females are smaller. Males also have an enlarged dorsal crest that often reaches its greatest height on the tail. Males are mottled brown, typically with contrasting gray diamonds dorsally. The throat fan may be just about any color from brown to yellow to red—even blue. It is often found around human habitations and likes sunny open areas. Care as for the green anole, but less fussy about humidity levels. Mixes fairly well with other anole species of similar size, but males are intolerant of other males of their own species (what else is new?). Food is insects.

The crested anole, *Anolis cristatellus*. Photo by R. D. Bartlett.

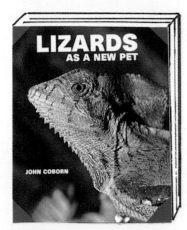

TU-025, 64 pages, 50+ color photos

PS-316, 128 pages, 50+ color photos

KW-196, 128 pages, 100+ color photos

PS-876, 384 pages, 175 color photos

KW-197, 128 pages, 110 color photos

TW-115, 256 pages, 180 photos

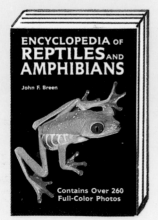

4-935, 576 pages, 260 color photos

SK-015, 64 pages, 50+ color photos

PS-311, 96 pages, 47 color photos

...From T.F.H., the world's largest publisher of bird books,
a new bird magazine for birdkeepers all over the world...

CAGED BIRD HOBBYIST
IS FOR EVERYONE
WHO LOVES BIRDS.

CAGED BIRD HOBBYIST
IS PACKED WITH VALUABLE
INFORMATION SHOWING HOW
TO FEED, HOUSE, TRAIN AND CARE
FOR ALL TYPES OF BIRDS.

Subscribe right now so you don't miss a single copy!

SM-316